29 Spanish Interactive Alphabet Mini-Books

Easy-to-make Reproducible Books That Promote Literacy

 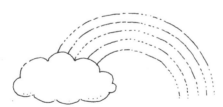 

by Mary Beth Spann

SCHOLASTIC PROFESSIONAL BOOKS

New York • Toronto • London • Auckland • Sydney • Buenos Aires

Scholastic Inc. grants teachers permission to photocopy the mini-book pages from this book for classroom use. No other part of this publication may be reproduced in whole or in part, or stored in a retrieval system, or transmitted in any form or by any means, electronic, mechanical, photocopying, or otherwise, without written permission of the publisher. For information regarding permission, write to Scholastic Inc., 555 Broadway, New York, NY 10012.

Cover design by Vincent Ceci and Jaime Lucero
Cover illustration by James G. Hale

Interior design by Sydney Wright
Interior illustrations by James G. Hale

ISBN 0-439-24442-0

Copyright © 2001 by Mary Beth Spann. All rights reserved. Printed in the U.S.A.
12 11 10 9 8   8 9/0

Contents

A B C ChDEFGH IJKLLlMNÑ OPQRS TUVWX YZ

About This Book 4

Directions For Printing, Folding and Cutting
Mini-Books 4

Ideas for Introducing Alphabet Mini-Books 5

What To Do With Completed Mini-Books 9

29 Spanish Interactive Alphabet Mini-Books . . .11

About This Book

29 Spanish Interactive Alphabet Mini-Books features a charming collection of reproducible alphabet mini-books that beginning readers will love to make, use, learn from, and collect. There is one mini-book for each letter of the Spanish alphabet. They are easy to copy, fold and cut, and equally easy for children to complete and enjoy. The books provide a fun-filled introduction to learning letter sounds and configurations, while inviting children to become acquainted with words beginning with each letter sound. They make a wonderful addition to your existing balanced language arts program as they support your efforts to provide a varied, print-rich classroom environment.

Directions for Printing, Folding, and Cutting Mini-Books

How-to Steps:

1. Make a double-sided copy of the mini-book pages. Start by making a copy of the first page of the mini-book with the title page in the lower left-hand corner of the platen glass.

2. Place this copy into the paper tray with the blank side up. Again, check to be sure that the title page appears in the lower left-hand corner. Then place the second page on the platen glass with page 2 (the letter collection) in the upper left-hand corner.

If your machine has a double-sided function and you wish to make copies that way, you will need to remove the mini-book pages from the book. Regardless of how you make the double-sided copies, you may need to experiment a bit to be sure that the pages are aligned properly and that page 2 appears behind the title page.

3. Cut the page in half along the dotted line.

4. Stack the pages so that page 3 appears behind the title page.

5. Fold the pages in half along the solid line. Once you've checked to be sure that the pages are in the proper order, staple them together along the book's spine.

Ideas for Introducing Alphabet Mini-Books

Begin by providing each child with a copy of the letter book you wish to complete. Read through the book together. Call children's attention to the page numbers featured on each page, and the labeled pictures presented on pages 5–7 in each mini-book. Invite students to color these pictures and the target letter as you complete the book together.

What follows is a page-by-page description of each mini-book followed by an extension activity you may want to try as you and your students complete each page. (Tip: Depending on your class, you may need to assemble the mini-books yourself before presenting them to your students.)

Mini-Book Title Page:

Directions: Each child writes his or her name in the space provided to personalize the book.

Aim: By personalizing each letter book, the child takes "ownership" of the work inside.

Extension Activity: Use a bulletin board to post individual self-portraits or photographs of the children. Each time a student completes a letter book, invite him or

her to display it beneath the corresponding picture. Or, post the pictures in a row so as to create a wall border. Then, as each student completes the particular letter book that begins his or her own name, have the students hang their own letter book beneath their picture.

**Mini-Book Page 2:
Letter Collection**

Directions: Children explore the target letter in different fonts.

Aim: To help children realize that letters can be formed in different fonts.

Extension Activity: Use a computer word processing program to help children print out and read letters in various font styles.

**Mini-Book Page 3:
My Letter Collection**

Directions: Children glue down examples of the target letter clipped or torn from newspapers and magazines.

Aim: To expose children to print as it appears in the world around them, for example on cereal boxes, on neighborhood signs, and in books, magazines, and newspapers.

Extension Activity: Have children create large scale letter collages by clipping individual letters from printed matter and gluing them to oaktag which has been precut into large alphabet letter shapes.

Mini-Book Page 4:

Directions: Children use their fingers then pencils to trace over upper and lowercase outlines of the target letter, then print the same letters on the lines below.

Aim: This page gives children guided printing practice, plus a chance to try printing letters without line constraints.

Extension Activity: Support children's need for tactile learning by having them trace letters in various mediums (finger paint, sand, rice, cereal, etc.). Also, provide bendable materials such as pipe cleaners, clay, and aluminum foil for children to mold into letter shapes.

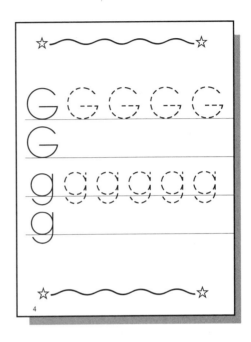

Mini-Book Pages 5, 6, and 7:

Directions: Children identify and color labeled objects that begin with the target letter.

Aim: Children will begin building a vocabulary of words beginning with a particular letter of the alphabet.

Extension Activity: Provide students with a flannel board and alphabet letters cut from assorted pieces of felt. Then try the following:

- Allow children time to play freely with the letters.
- Show them how they may use the letters to spell out words they encounter around the classroom or in books or magazines.
- Have each child locate the first letter of his or her name.
- Place two or more letters on the board and play a guessing game using different criteria. (E.g., I'm thinking of a letter that is composed of a tall stick and a circle shape. It is also the letter that is at the beginning of the word "doll.")
- Have children take turns coming up to the board and closing their eyes. As the class looks on, help the participating child trace the shape of a letter with his or her fingers and then attempt to guess which letter it is.

**Mini-Book Page 8:
My Letter Word Bank**

Directions: Children use the space provided to write and/or draw new words beginning with the target letter. They can either write or illustrate the words themselves, or they can cut and paste photos or illustrations of words that begin with the target letter.

Aim: This page encourages children to dip into their own experiences as they choose favorite and familiar words to feature.

Extension Activity: Help children label their illustrations. Also, take time to share children's word collections with the rest of the class. Use chart pad paper to record all the words the class generated for each letter. Consider printing each word onto a separate piece of manila paper and binding these pages into a picture dictionary, with children supplying the illustrations and definitions, if desired.

What to Do With Completed Mini-books

Here are some ideas for getting the most out of your completed mini-books:

Book Rings

Give each child a loose-leaf binder ring on which to collect their books. Store the rings in a box; allow the children to take the rings home after each mini-book addition, or when all the letters books are complete. (Tip: Pipe cleaners bent into circle shapes with the ends twisted together can double as inexpensive "ring" substitutes.)

Mini-Book Masterpieces

Glue each mini-book to the center of a piece of construction paper. Use the border of the construction paper (instead of page 8 of the mini-book) as a Word Bank space

9

to glue or draw and label alphabet pictures. Assemble each child's mounted mini-book in alphabetical order and then bind each set together between oaktag covers to create individual alphabet books for children to treasure.

Alphabet Quilts

Have each child turn their books into an alphabet pocket quilt. Enlist a parent's help in cutting business-size envelopes (saved from junk mail) in half to make "pockets." Arrange 29 pockets onto a piece of oaktag, and glue in place. Reinforce each pocket with clear tape and label them with an alphabet letter. Then, as children complete their mini-books, they may slip each one into its own little paper pocket. If you wish, use wide heavy-duty packing tape to secure a metal hanger to the top (back side) of each quilt so children may hang their creations up in class or at home. (Tip: To lend stability to the oaktag, tape the hanger onto the quilt back so that only the hanger hook extends above the top edge. You may want to wrap sharp hanger hook ends with packing tape to avoid injury.)

Shoe Box Treasure Chests

Ask each student to bring a shoe box to class. Have students create hinged tops for their boxes by taping one of the lid's long sides to the box. If necessary, use a scissors to snip the corners of each box lid apart so that it lifts freely. Cover the boxes and lids with light colored craft paper. Then, have children trace or print alphabet letters onto the paper. Trace the shapes with glue and sprinkle them with glitter. Have students use these boxes as treasure chests for collecting and storing completed mini-books.

Culminating Letter Book Celebration

You may wish to mark the completion of your letter book project by inviting family members in to view the books and celebrate your accomplishment with you. Here are some easy-to-execute ideas to make this party a success:

- Invite children to pick a favorite alphabet mini-book to "read" to the group.
- Prepare other simple alphabet activities to share, such as a rendition of the ABC song, or a walk-through display of related alphabet books, crafts, writing samples and projects.
- Serve alphabet inspired refreshments such as "iced-T", Hi-C™, and homemade cookies cut into letter shapes.

Page 5

aguja

abrigo

Page 8

Mi banco de palabras con la letra Aa

Page 4

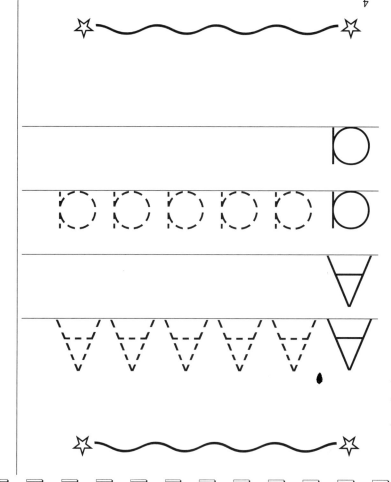

Page 1

El libro de la letra Aa

de _____

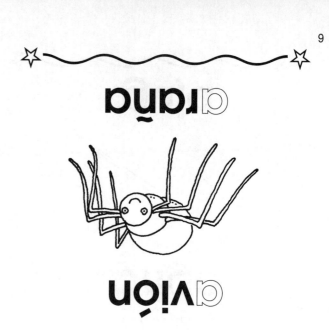
araña

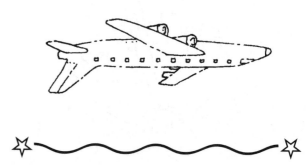
avión

Mi colección de letras Aa

Colección de letras Aa

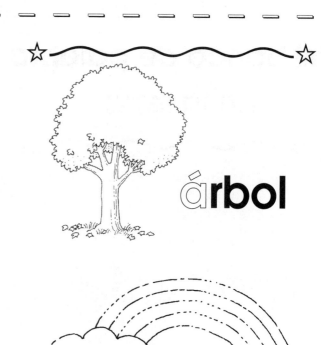
árbol

arco iris

Page 5

bellota

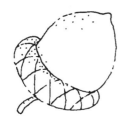

bola

Page 8

Mi banco de palabras con la letra **Bb**

Page 4

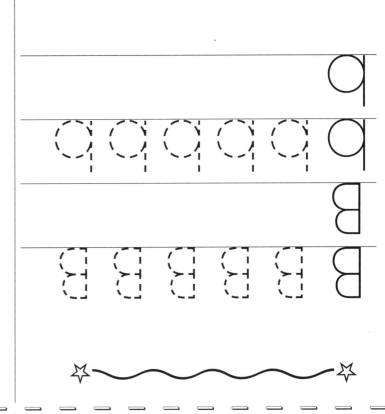

Page 1

El libro de la letra **Bb**

de _____

3

bizcocho

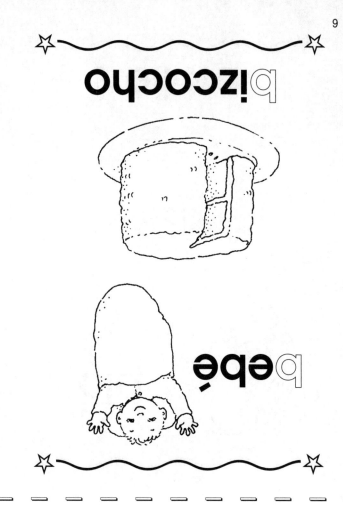

bebé

Mi colección
de letras Bb

buzón

botón

Colección de letras Bb

Page 5

Conejo

Cocodrilo

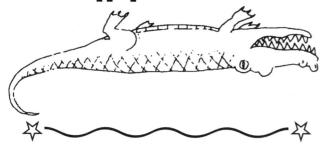

Page 4

Page 8

Mi banco de palabras con la letra Cc

Page 1

El libro de la letra

Cc

de _____

Colección de letras Cc

Mi colección de letras Cc

camión

calabaza

casa

calcetines

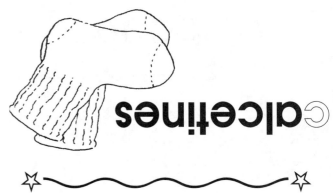

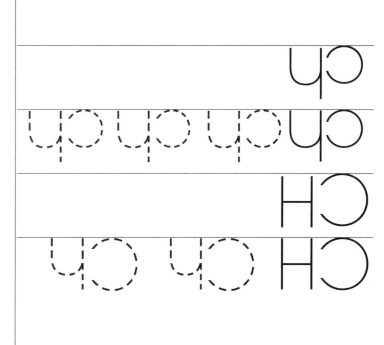

Chancleta

Chaqueta

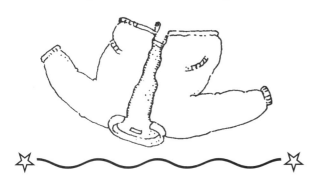

Mi banco de palabras con las letras Ch ch

El libro de las letras

Ch ch

de _____

Colección de letras Ch ch

Ch Ch ch Ch Ch ch

Mi colección de letras Ch ch

charca

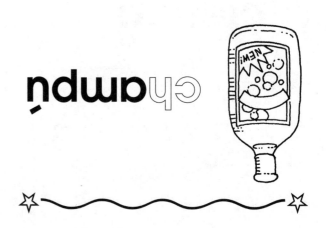

champú

chile

pecho

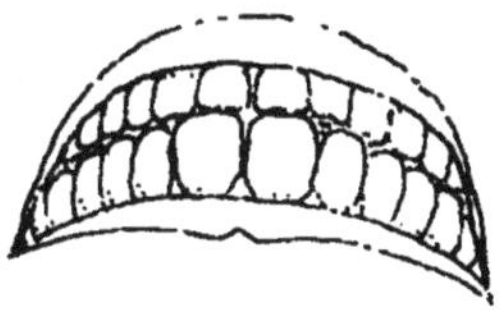

dientes

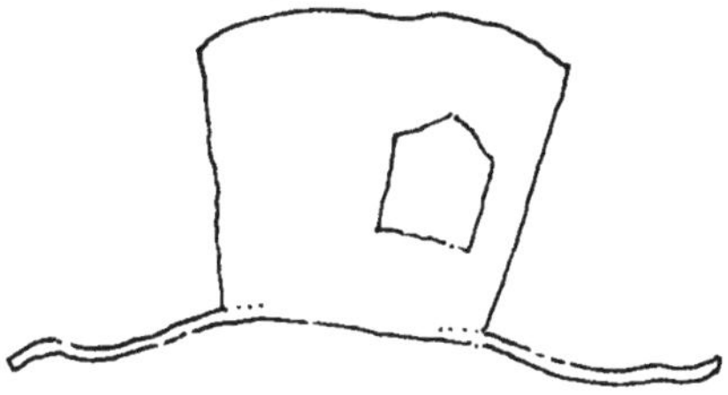

delantal

D D D D D D

D

d d d d d d

d

Mi banco de palabras con la letra Dd

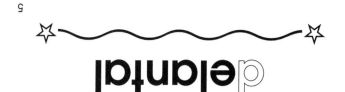

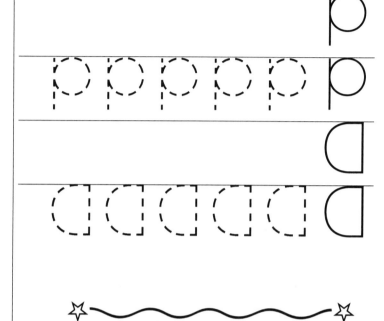

El libro de la letra Dd

de ____________

Colección de letras Dd

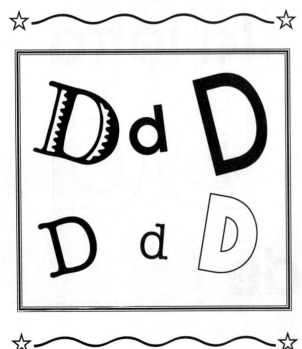

Mi colección de letras Dd

---

dentrífico

dulces

---

dedo

dinosaurio

El libro de la letra

Ee

de _____

Mi banco de palabras con la letra Ee

estrella de mar

elefante

Colección de letras Ee

Mi colección de letras Ee

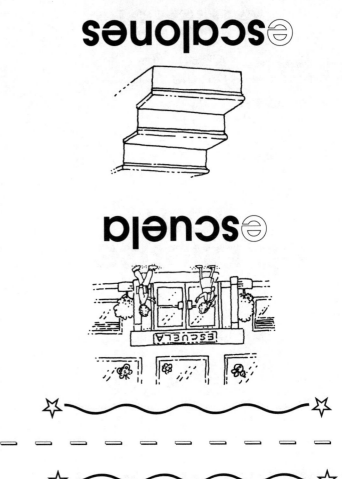

escuela

escalones

espejo

embudo

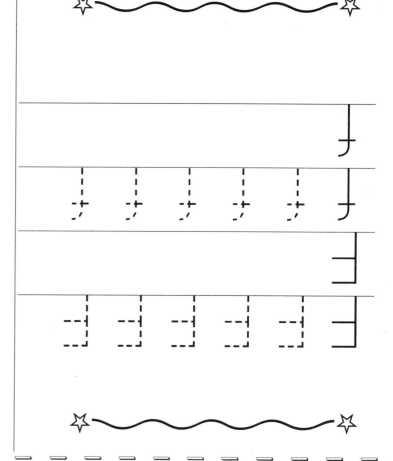

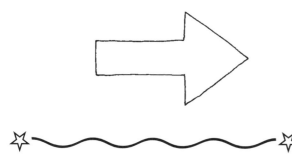

flor

flecha

Mi banco de palabras con la letra Ff

El libro de la letra

Ff

de _____

Colección de letras Ff

Mi colección de letras Ff

foca

falda

faro

flauta

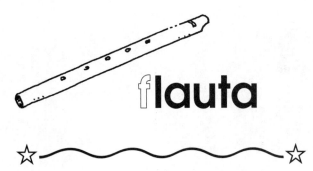

Mi banco de palabras con la letra

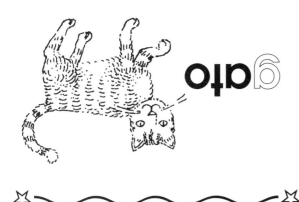

gato

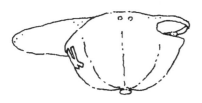

gorra

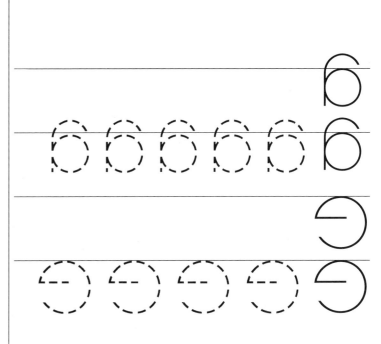

El libro de la letra

de _____

Colección de letras Gg

Mi colección de letras Gg

gafas
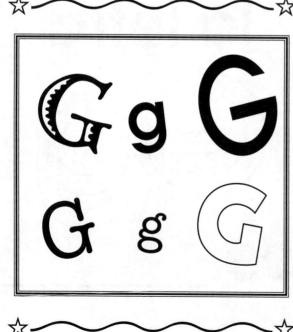

gancho de ropa

goma de mascar

guantes
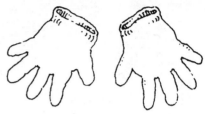

El libro de la letra Hh

de _____

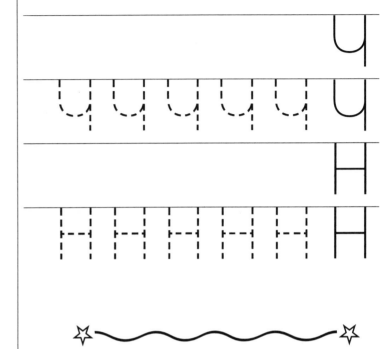

Mi banco de palabras con la letra Hh

hipopótamo

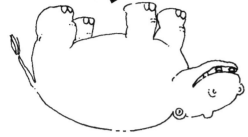

helado

Colección de letras Hh

Mi colección de letras Hh

h**ormiga**

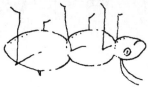

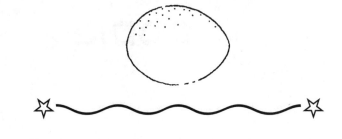
h**uevo**

h**oja**

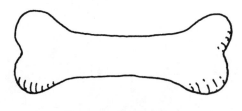
h**ueso**

El libro de la letra

Ii

de _____

Mi banco de palabras con la letra Ii

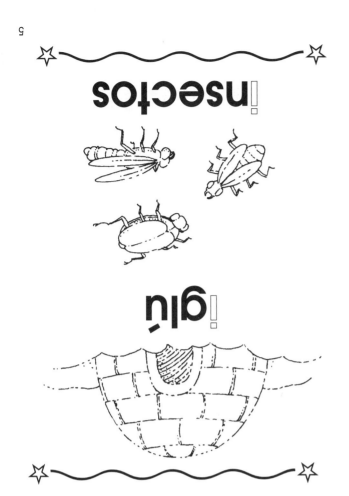

¡iglú

¡insectos

¡iguana!

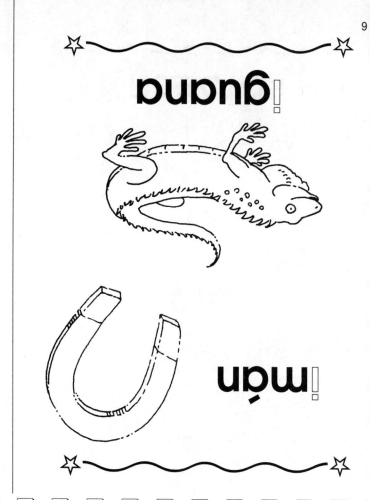

¡imán!

Mi colección de letras Ii

Colección de letras Ii

isla

impermeable

Page 5

¡jarrón

¡jabón

Page 8

Mi banco de palabras con la letra Jj

Page 4

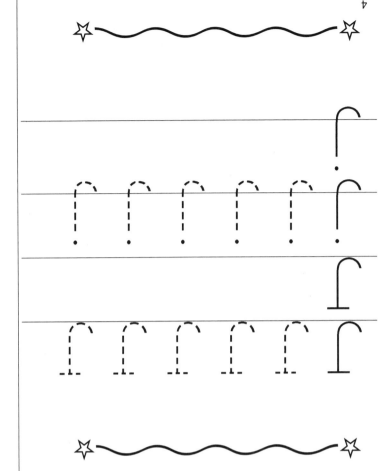

Page 1

El libro de la letra

Jj

de _____

Colección de letras Jj

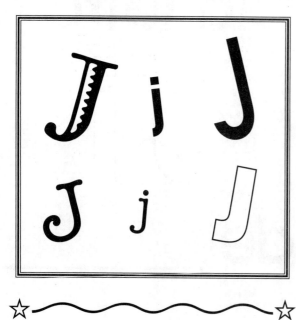

Mi colección de letras Jj

jaula

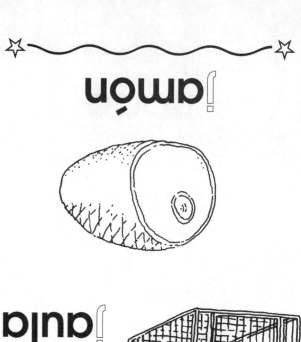

jamón

jirafa

jaguar

Mi banco de palabras con la letra Kk

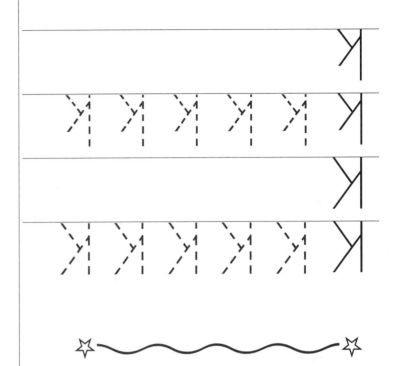

El libro de la letra

Kk

de _____

Colección de letras Kk

Mi colección de letras Kk

kiosco

kárate

kayak

koala

El libro de la letra

Ll

de _____

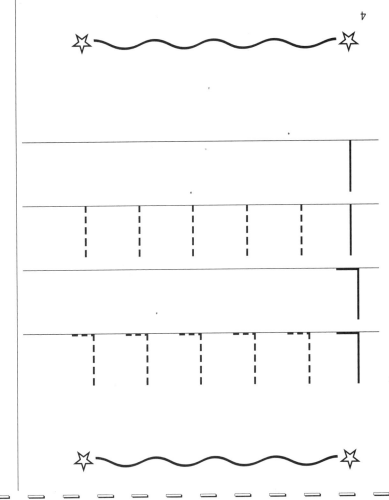

Mi banco de palabras con la letra Ll

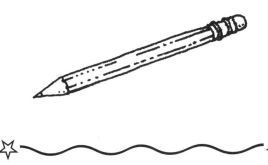

lápiz

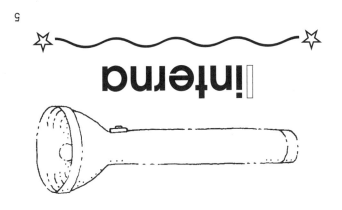

linterna

Colección de letras Ll

Mi colección de letras Ll

limones

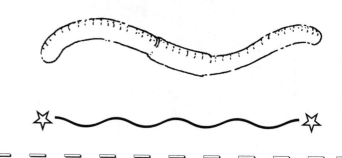

lechuza

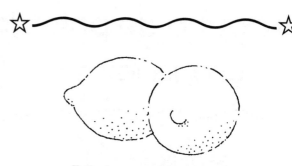

---

lombriz

león

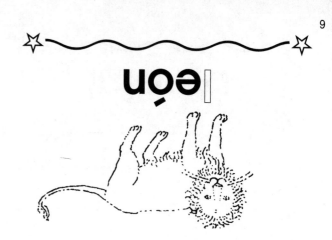

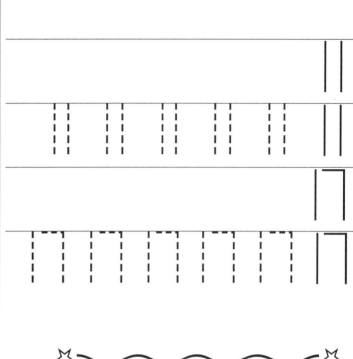

El libro de las letras
Ll ll
de _____

llave

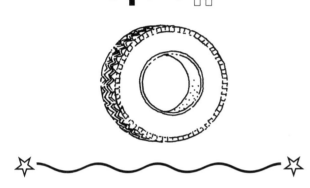

llanta

Mi banco de palabras con las letras Ll ll

Colección de letras Ll

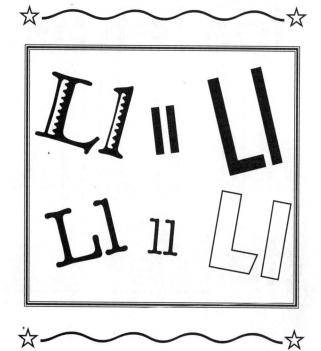

Mi colección de letras Ll

mantequilla

caballo

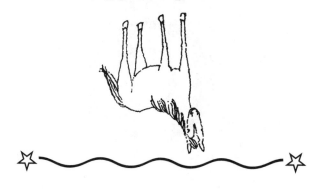

lluvia

llama

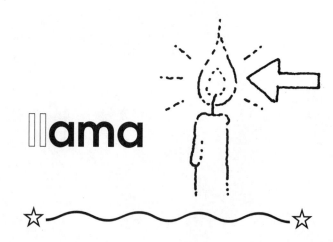

El libro de la letra

Mm

de _____

Mi banco de palabras con la letra M m

 manzana

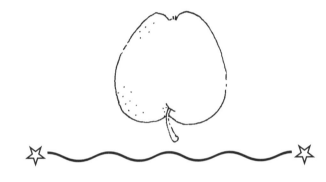 murciélago

Colección de letras Mm

Mi colección de letras Mm

m**apache**

m**ano**
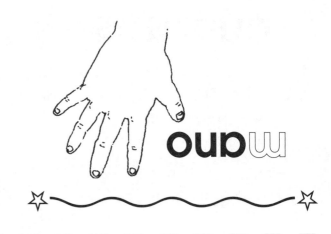

m**itón**

m**áscara**

Page 5

n**ido**

n**aranja**

Page 8

Mi banco de palabras con la letra N n

Page 4

Page 1

El libro de la letra

Nn

de _____

Colección de letras Nn

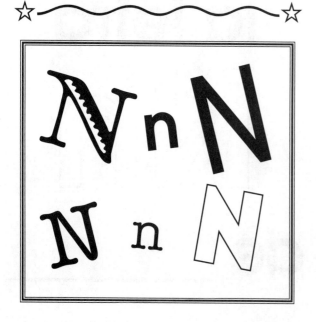

Mi colección de letras Nn

n**ariz**

n**ube**

n**udo**

n**uez**

El libro de la letra Ññ de _____

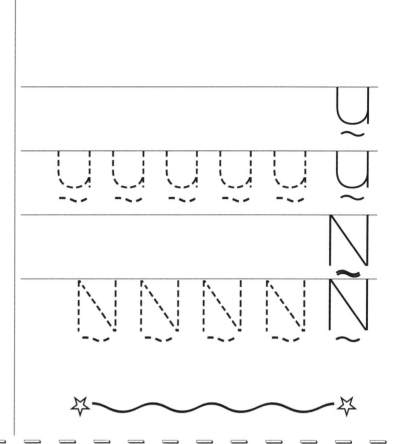

Mi banco de palabras con la letra Ññ

niña

telaraña

cumpleaños

pañuelo

Mi colección
de letras Ññ

Colección de letras Ññ

sueño

muñeca

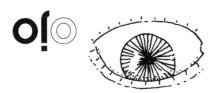 ojo

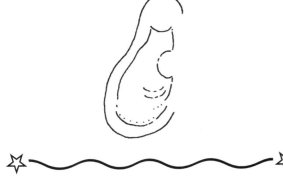 oreja

Mi banco de palabras con la letra Oo

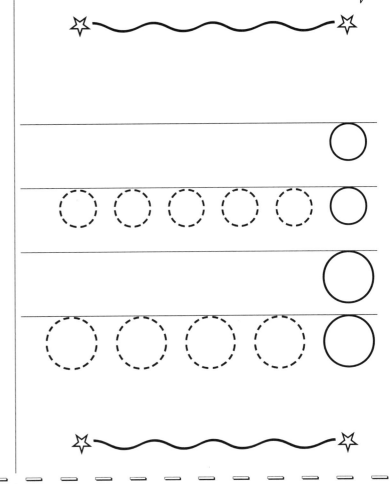

El libro de la letra Oo

de _____

Colección de letras ○○

Mi colección de letras ○○

○stra

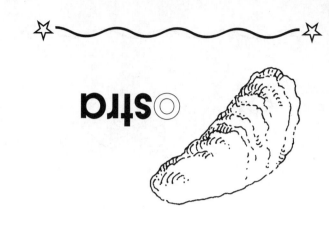

○lla

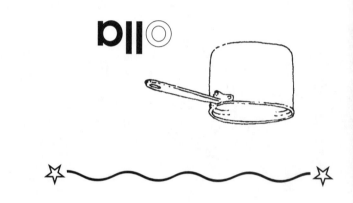

○villo

○ruga

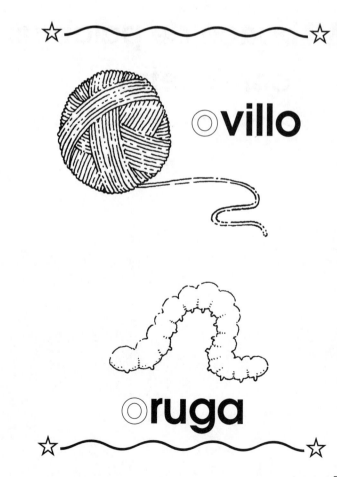

El libro de la letra Pp

de _____

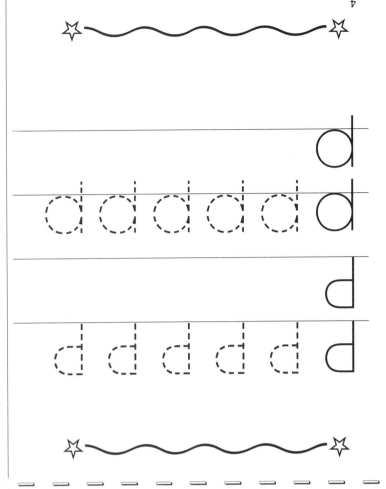

Mi banco de palabras con la letra Pp

pato

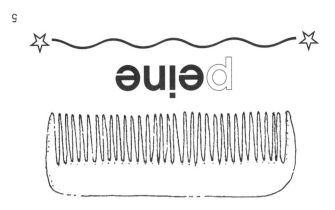

peine

Colección de letras Pp

P p P p P

Mi colección de letras Pp

puerta

perro

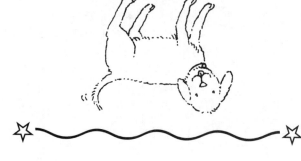

pluma

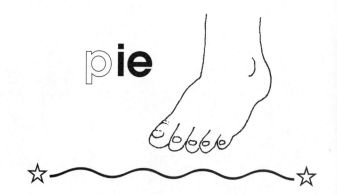
pie

El libro de la letra Qq

de _____

Mi banco de palabras con la letra Qq

queso

quijada

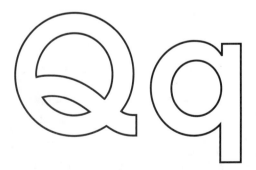

orquídea

mariquita

Mi colección de letras Qq

Colección de letras Qq

raqueta

15 quince

Mi banco de palabras con la letra Rr

rana

ratón

El libro de la letra

Rr

de _____

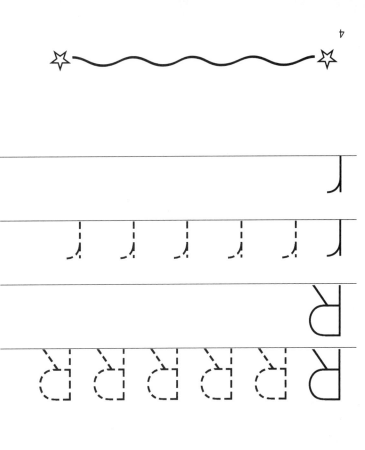

Colección de letras Rr

Mi colección de letras Rr

r**eina**

r**ey**

r**ueda**

r**obot**

saltamontes

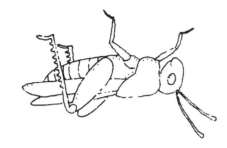

sobre

Mi banco de palabras con la letra Ss

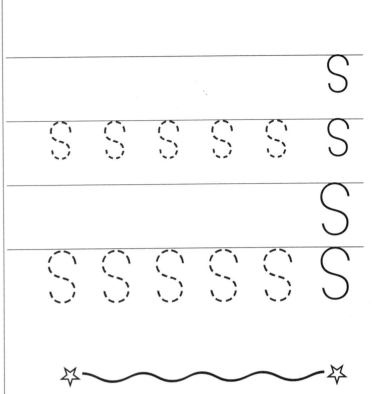

El libro de la letra

Ss

de _____

Colección de letras Ss

Mi colección de letras Ss

s**ortija**

s**ol**

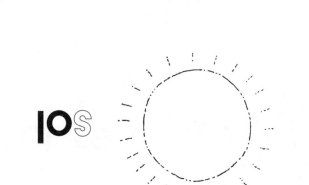

s**uéter**

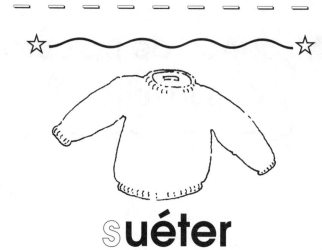

s**igno de pregunta**

tronco

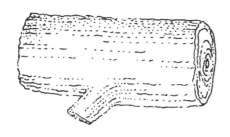

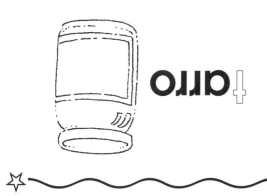

tarro

Mi banco de palabras con la letra Tt

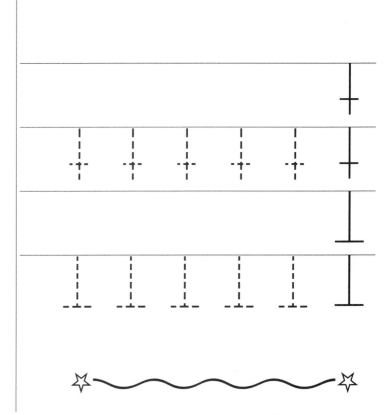

El libro de la letra

de _____

tigre

tortuga

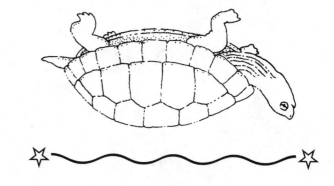

Mi colección de letras Tt

Colección de letras Tt

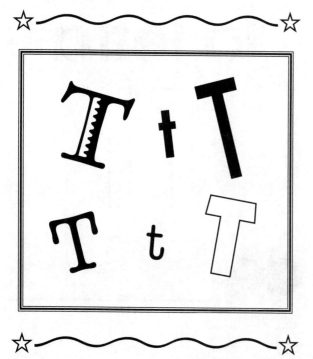

teléfono

televisión

Page 5 (upside down)

uniforme

uvas

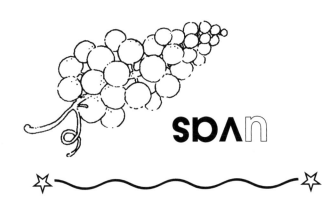

Page 8

Mi banco de palabras
con la letra Uu

Page 4

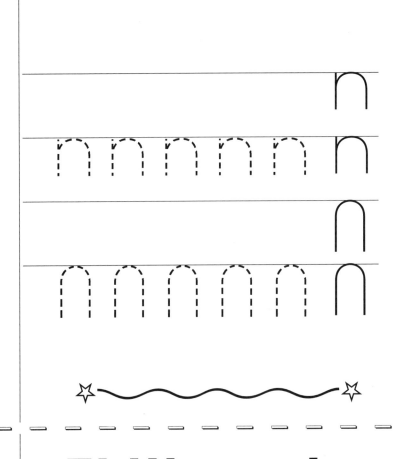

Page 1

El libro de
la letra

Uu

de _____

Colección de letras Uu

Mi colección de letras Uu

unicornio

uniciclo

uno

uña

Page 5

Viña

Vestido

Page 8

Mi banco de palabras con la letra Vv

Page 4

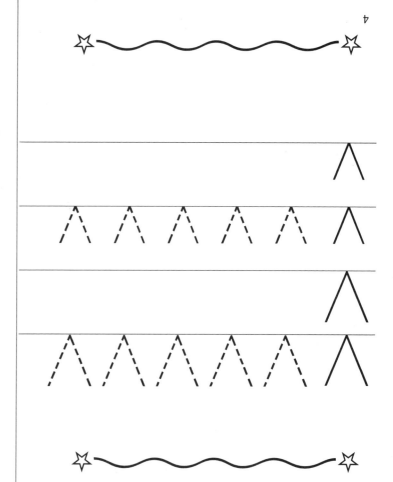

Page 1

El libro de la letra Vv

de _____

Colección de letras Vv

Mi colección de letras Vv

Ventana

Violín

Valla

Vaca

El libro de la letra Ww

de _____

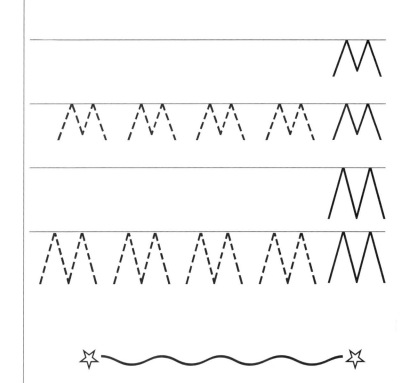

Waldo

Mi banco de palabras con la letra Ww

waffles

wapiti

Mi colección de letras Ww

Colección de letras Ww

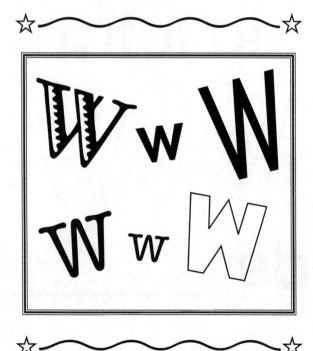

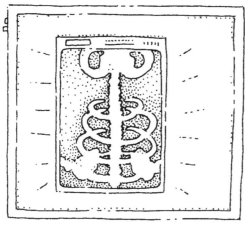

rayos X

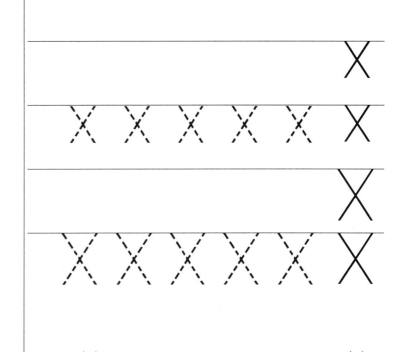

Mi banco de palabras con la letra Xx

El libro de la letra

Xx

de _____

Colección de letras Xx

- - - - - - - - - - - - - - - - - - -

Mi colección de letras Xx

Xilófono

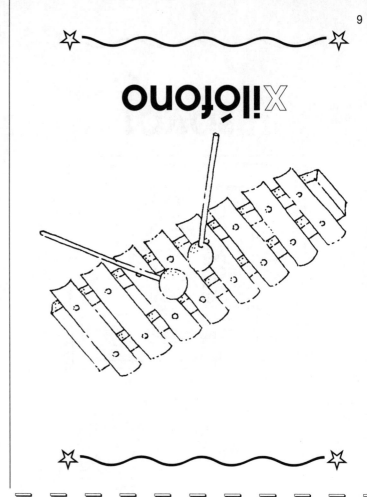

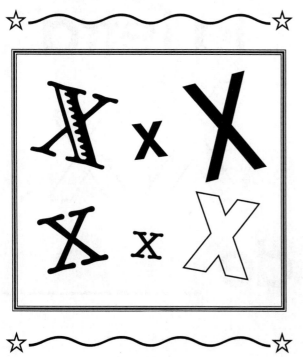

sa**x**ofón

[page 5]

Yogur

Yate

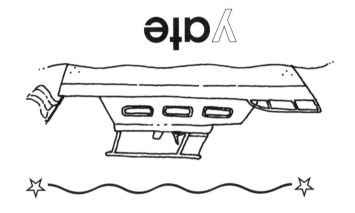

[page 4]

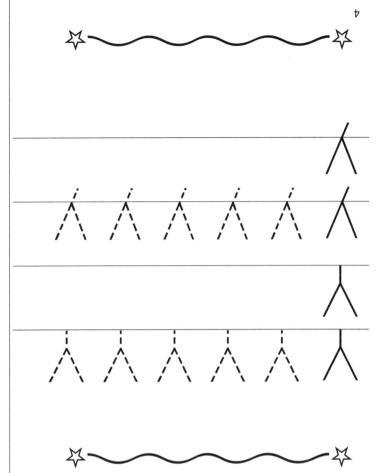

[page 8]

Mi banco de palabras con la letra Yy

[page 1]

El libro de la letra

Yy

de _____

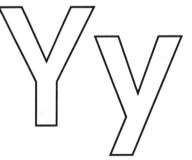

Colección de letras Yy

Mi colección de letras Yy

Yema de huevo

Yoyo

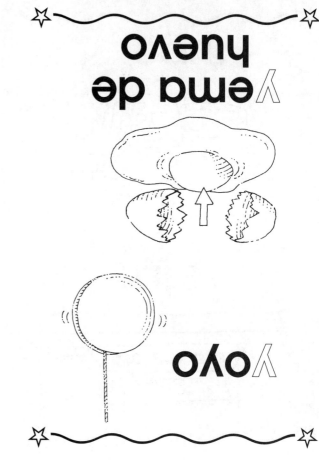

---

rayo

playa

zig zag

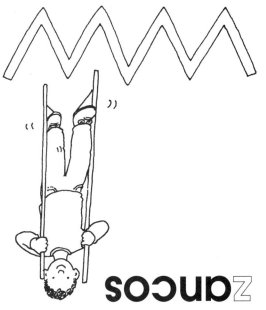

zancos

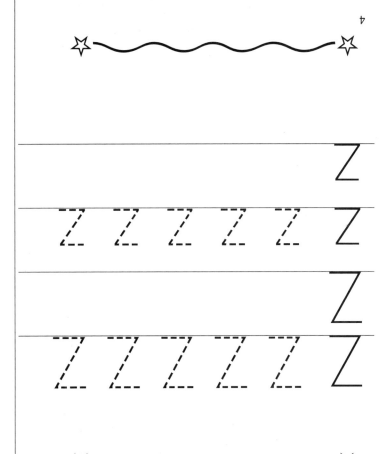

Mi banco de palabras con la letra Z z

El libro de la letra Zz

de _____

Colección de letras Zz

Mi colección de letras Zz

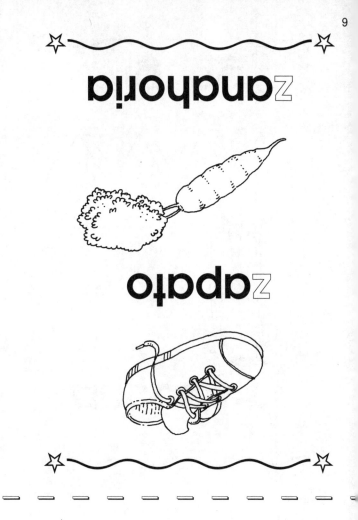

z**anahoria**

z**apato**

z**orro**

z**arpa**

_____

_____

_____

_____

_____

Mi banco de palabras con la letra ____

El libro de la letra

_____

de _____

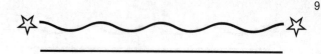

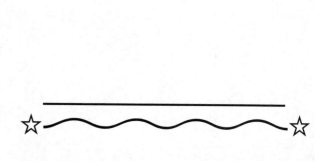

Mi colección de letras ___

Colección de letras ___

_____

_____

_____

_____

_____

_____

_____

_____

Mi banco de palabras con la letra ____

El libro de la letra

_____

de _____

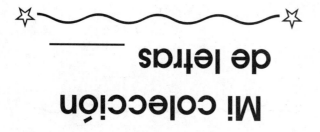

Colección de letras ___

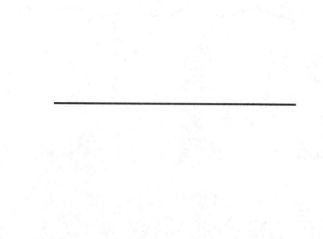

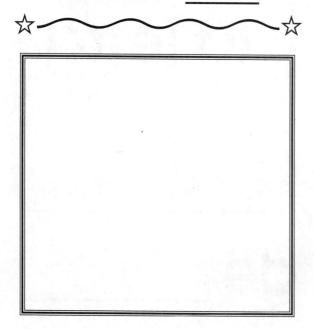